Exercises in Astronomical Data Analysis for Beginners

OrangeBooks Publication

Smriti Nagar, Bhilai, Chhattisgarh - 490020

Website:**www.orangebooks.in**

© Copyright, 2023, Dr. Smriti Mahajan
Email: mahajan.smriti@gmail.com

All rights reserved. No part of this book may be reproduced, stored in a retrieval system, or transmitted, in any form by any means, electronic, mechanical, magnetic, optical, chemical, manual, photocopying, recording or otherwise, without the prior written consent of its writer.

First Edition, 2023

EXERCISES IN ASTRONOMICAL DATA ANALYSIS FOR BEGINNERS

Smriti Mahajan

OrangeBooks Publication
www.orangebooks.in

Dedicated
to
my teachers and mentors

PREFACE

Astronomy is a fundamental science. It is crucial not only for understanding simple astronomical phenomenon such as eclipses, and the occurrence of day and night, but also for observing the laws of Physics in action. Advances in technology have opened up new realms of astronomy, and with it, fundamental Physics. This has allowed us to harness a small fraction of the information stored in the cosmos, and its intriguing patterns, through various ground and space-based facilities.

In many fields of science, and particularly in astronomy, a lot of data are now available on the internet for anybody to use. While popular textbooks of astronomy provide in-depth knowledge on various aspects of the field, and advanced books on individual topics are good for understanding fundamental Physics underlying astronomical observations, these are of limited use to a young student, or an uninitiated teacher who although interested in astronomy, are often confused about where to begin.

When I started teaching astronomy at IISER Mohali, I wanted to incorporate a practical session for the students where they worked with real data. My vision was simple: if they saw how the equations and formulae that they have learnt help astronomers in unraveling the Physics using real data, they will understand the concept better. However, the problem was that there were no help books for such exercises. While some of the standard textbooks provide handful of programming-based exercises, they assumed a certain level of prior knowledge of programming (often in a specific programming language), and were limited to advanced exercises. But since I was adamant in adding that practical session to my course, I started on a time consuming but rewarding journey of collecting datasets and designing exercises which could be completed by students with a range of expertise. These exercises assumed very basic understanding of computing, and helped students understand the "theory" better.

This book is a small collection of such exercises which will help bridge the gap between astronomy text books and practical research, by providing easy examples and problems based on publicly available data. This book is aimed at high school and college teachers, amateur astronomers and astronomy students. A basic understanding of astronomy and computing will come in handy, but is not necessary in performing these exercises since each chapter includes a brief summary of the concept and jargon.

The two-fold aim of this book is to introduce the learner to astronomical resources and provide basic insights into how beautiful images are used to generate quantitative data. These data in turn, aided by fundamental mathematics and understanding of physical phenomenon provide proof of theory, and help establish the elementary laws of nature.

Happy exploring!

TABLE OF CONTENT

Kepler's Law 1

Binary star systems 4

The stellar spectra.......................................9

Colour...14

Star clusters..20

Shapes of galaxies 23

Light profile of galaxies..............................26

Measuring Redshift of galaxies..................32

The Hubble law 36

Mass of a cluster 41

Mass of a galaxy 45

More Resources on the internet 50

An incomplete list of self study textbooks..............55

Some useful constants 56

KEPLER'S LAW

Johannes Kepler, the German astronomer presented the three laws governing planetary motion between 1609-1618. Kepler's laws were based on his analysis of the data collected by his danish colleague Tycho Brahe. Kepler's laws state that (i) All planets move around the sun in elliptical orbits with sun at one of the foci, (ii) The radius vector connecting the sun to the planet sweeps out equal areas in equal intervals of time, and (iii) the square of the orbital time period of planets is directly proportional to the cube of the semi-major axis of its orbit.

In this chapter we will concentrate on proving the Kepler's third law using data obtained from NASA. The mean distance of the planets relative to the Earth, and their orbital periods are provided in Table 1. In order to test Kepler's law, square the values in row 1 and cube the values in row 2, and plot them against one another to show that (distance)^2 $\propto$ (orbital period)^3 as shown in Figure 1.

Tip: It might be useful to use a log-log plot for this exercise, given the range of values along both axes.

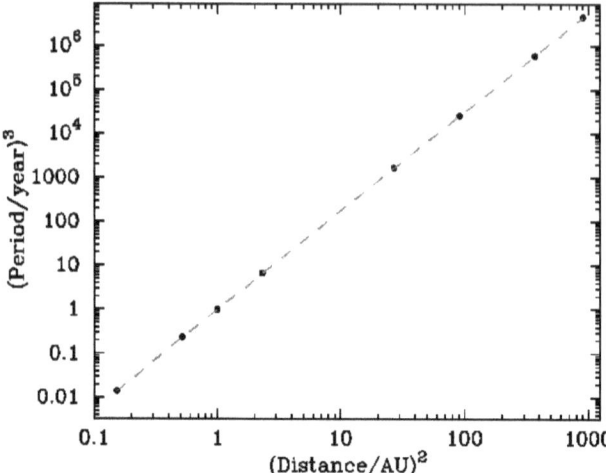

Figure 1: This plot is the proof of Kepler's third law of planetary motions based on observational data.

Table 1: The distance and orbital periods of all the planets in the solar system relative to earth.								
	Mercury	Venus	Earth	Mars	Jupiter	Saturn	Uranus	Neptune
Mean distance from Sun (in AU)	0.39	0.72	1.0	1.52	5.20	9.54	19.18	30.06
Orbital Period (Earth years)	0.24	0.62	1.0	1.88	11.86	29.46	84.01	164.80

Exercise: Besides planets there are several dwarf planets orbiting the sun. The key difference between a planet and a dwarf planet is that the latter have not cleared their orbit, i.e. there are similar sized objects in their orbits which are also orbiting the sun. Pluto, for instance, is a dwarf planet. Although five dwarf planets mentioned below are recognised by NASA, there are apparently hundreds of them waiting to be discovered.

The data for nine dwarf planets in the solar system are provided in Table 2. Repeat the above exercise to check if the Kepler's law applies to them as well.

Table 2: The distance and orbital periods of nine dwarf planets in the solar system relative to earth.									
	Ceres	Orcus	Pluto	Haumea	Quaoar	Makemake	Gonggong	Eris	Sedna
Mean distance from Sun (in AU)	2.77	39.40	39.48	43.22	43.69	45.56	67.38	67.38	506.8
Orbital Period (Earth years)	4.60	247.3	247.9	284.1	288.8	307.5	553.1	558.0	approx. 11400

BINARY STAR SYSTEMS

Measuring fundamental parameters such as mass, radius etc. for individual stars can be very difficult given their point-like size and (mostly) faint luminosity. But nature has provided a solution to this problem in the form of multiple star systems. It is believed that at least half of all the stars in our galaxy are multiple-star systems, i.e. two or more stars orbiting a common centre of mass. For instance, Sirius, the brightest star in the night sky is a binary system made up of a bright Sun-like star and a much fainter companion star.

For convenience, we will only concentrate on binary star systems here. Binaries, depending upon the method of detection can be further segregated into different sub-categories. Some of these are:

Optical/Apparent binaries: These are stars which appear to be close together on the sky, but are not gravitationally bound to each other.

Visual/Astrometric binaries: Both the stars of the binary system are well distinguished from each other. Sirius is a well known example!

Eclipsing binaries: The orbital plane of this system is along the line of sight (or close to it), such that one star appears

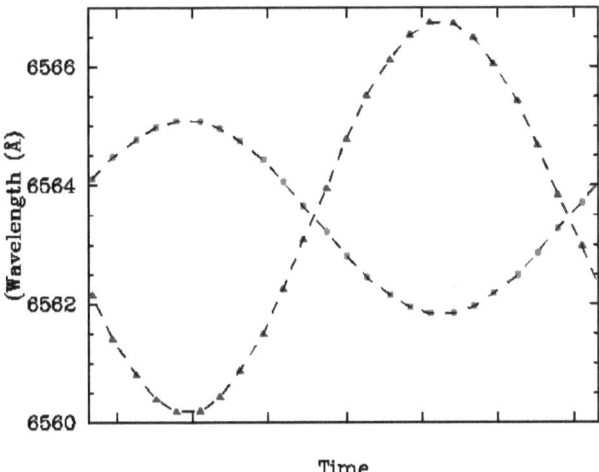

Figure 2: The variation in the wavelength of Hydrogen alpha line (6563 Å) for two components of a binary system (points and triangles, respectively) as they move around the common centre of mass.

to block the light from the other (aka "eclipse") as they move in their orbits around a common centre of mass.

Spectroscopic binaries: These star systems are detected via change in their spectra. The spectrum taken at different times show spectral lines that shift back and forth in wavelength as the two stars move around their common centre of mass. Data for one such system are shown in Figure 2 and provided in Table 3. By estimating the time period of the binary system and its mean velocity, the mass of the system can be evaluated as:

$$M = M_1 + M_2 = \frac{T}{2\pi G} \frac{(v_1 + v_2)^3}{sin^3 i},$$

where, M and T are the total mass and time period of the system, v_1 and v_2 are the velocities of component stars, G is the gravitational constant and l is the angle between the line-of-sight and the plane of the binary system. For an ideal eclipsing binary system, $l = 90°$. Also, it is trivial to show that for components 1 and 2, $\frac{m_1}{m_2} = \frac{v_2}{v_1} = \frac{r_2}{r_1}$.

It is notable that the same star system can be a specimen for more than one categories discussed above.

Exercise: Table 3 provides wavelengths for Hydrogen alpha (Hα) lines as observed for the two components of a star system at different instances. Assuming the rest-frame wavelength of the Hα line to be 6562.08 Å,

- Plot a time vs velocity curve for this eclipsing binary system.

- Determine the masses of the components of the binary.

- Stars on the main sequence (MS) attain equilibrium by fusing Hydrogen into Helium. Our Sun is a MS star. Read more about MS at https://www.atnf.csiro.au/outreach/education/senior/astrophysics/stellarevolution_mainsequence.html. The main sequence is often observed between luminosity (or absolute magnitude) and temperature (or spectral class). This plane, called the Hertzsprung-Russell (HR) diagram determines the evolutionary sequence of a star based on its observed properties. Read more about the HR diagram at https://www.atnf.csiro.au/outreach//education/senior/astrophysics/stellarevolution_hrintro.html.
  Assuming both the stars are present on the MS, find their spectral types.

Table 3: Data for spectroscopic binary system.

Time (Julian date)	Line 1 (Å)	Line 2 (Å)
243866.01	6564.114	6562.150
243866.09	6564.480	6561.410
243866.18	6564.777	6560.811
243866.26	6564.984	6560.392
243866.34	6565.088	6560.183
243866.43	6565.081	6560.197
243866.51	6564.963	6560.434
243866.59	6564.744	6560.878
243866.68	6564.437	6561.498
243866.76	6564.064	6562.252
243866.84	6563.650	6563.088
243866.93	6563.224	6563.951
243867.01	6562.813	6564.780
243867.09	6562.448	6565.519
243867.18	6562.151	6566.119
243867.26	6561.944	6566.537
243867.34	6561.841	6566.746
243867.43	6561.848	6566.731
243867.51	6561.965	6566.494

Table 3: Data for spectroscopic binary system.

Time (Julian date)	Line 1 (Å)	Line 2 (Å)
243867.59	6562.185	6566.050
243867.68	6562.492	6565.430
243867.76	6562.865	6564.676
243867.84	6563.279	6563.839
243867.93	6563.706	6562.977
243868.01	6564.116	6562.148

THE STELLAR SPECTRA

Besides images, the energy output of astronomical objects can be measured using a spectrum. A spectrum is the distribution of photon energies emitted by an object as a function of wavelength (or frequency). Most stars can be approximated as perfect black bodies. As a result, the peak wavelength of a star's spectrum correlates with its surface temperature according to Wien's law. Besides temperature, the spectrum also tells us about the chemical composition and the distance of the object from us.

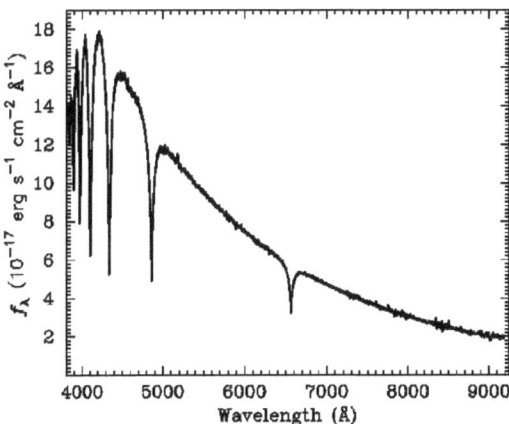

Figure 3: A stellar spectra is often characterised by absorption lines of varying depth. (Data source: SDSS)

The modern classification of stellar spectra is provided on the basis of decreasing surface temperature in the sequence OBAFGKM (mnemonic to remember: *"Oh Be A Fine Girl/Guy Kiss Me"*). This is called the Harvard classification scheme created by the American astronomer Annie Jump Cannon, by rearranging some of the earlier classification schemes[1] available to her. The table below provides some key spectral characteristics for each of the spectral classes, going from the hottest blue stars to the coolest red ones.

	Table 4: Prominent features in stellar spectra	
Spectral Type	**Temperature (Kelvin)**	**Prominent spectral lines**
O	28,000-50,000	Ionised Helium
B	10,000-28,000	Helium, some Hydrogen
A	7500-10,000	Strong hydrogen, some ionised metals
F	6000-7500	Hydrogen, ionised calcium (labelled as H and K), iron
G	5000-6000	Neutral and ionised metals, especially Calcium, strong G band
K	3500-5000	Neutral metals, sodium

---

[1] *It is interesting to note that when Cannon published her classification scheme in 1901, its physical basis was unknown and remained a mystery for several years. Cannon further classified around 200,000 spectra between 1911-14 which are recorded in the Henry-Draper catalogue. To date, many stars are known by their HD number. In 1921, Cannon became the first woman to receive a doctor of Astronomy degree from the Groningen University. Later, she was also presented with an honorary degree from the Oxford University.*

Exercises in Astronomical Data Analysis for Beginners

Table 4: Prominent features in stellar spectra		
Spectral Type	Temperature (Kelvin)	Prominent spectral lines
M	2500-3500	Strong titanium oxide, very strong sodium

Exercise 1: Let us try to classify some stellar spectra[2] using data from the Sloan Digital Sky survey (SDSS).

- Go to https://dr14.sdss.org/optical/spectrum/view and access the spectra using the information provided in the table below.

Table 5: SDSS ID for stellar spectra.			
Plate/MJD	Fiber	Plate/MJD	Fiber
266/51630	21	266/51630	513
273/51597	2	273/51597	157
281/51614	4	281/51614	133
498/51984	538	273/51597	589

- Once the spectrum loads, identify the strongest spectral lines and make a list. The observed spectrum is plotted along with a model spectrum (often shown in red), which is used to measure the redshift of this object by the SDSS pipeline. It is possible to zoom into the spectrum simply by selecting a rectangular region

---

[2] *This exercise is inspired from the projects for students provided by the SDSS at https://skyserver.sdss.org/dr14/en/proj/advanced/spectraltypes/spectraltypeshome.aspx*

around it. Double clicking on the spectrum will zoom out to the full spectrum again.

- Can you spot any similar features between different stars? Are there any common features between some of the stars? Try to group them together and note down their most prominent spectral features. Then go back to the previous step and repeat the exercise for a more robust classification. Repeat these steps until you are confident about your classification scheme.

- Compare your list of prominent features for each group of stars with the spectral classification provided in Table 4 and try to identify the spectral class for your stars.

Exercise 2: Let us classify some more stellar spectra.

- Launch the plate browser using this link https://skyserver.sdss.org/dr14/en/tools/getimg/plate.aspx.

- Choose any plate, and click on 'get plate'. This will show a table of various objects observed on that plate. Choose any number of stars from the table and try to identify their spectral type. Note that you may not be able to get all the spectral classes in a single plate, and there may be more than one stars of a class. Beware! Some spectral classes are difficult to tell apart.

- If you have performed the above exercise for a few tens of stars, plot a histogram showing the number of stars you got for each of the classes OBAFGKM. Is there any trend here? Which type of stars are most common? Which are least common? Are there any stars which remain unclassifiable?

Some key points that you must consider for these exercises are:

i. In general, O stars are rare because they are very short lived. In fact, the life span of stars decreases with increasing temperature.

ii. We have discussed only the most well known spectral classes here. However, there are other low temperature classes which were discovered later, e.g. carbon stars, brown dwarfs (Type L and Type T stars), Wolf-rayet stars (Type W) etc., which are very rare.

iii. Occasionally a star may be at the boundary of two classes and hence difficult to classify by looking at the spectra alone.

COLOUR

In astronomy, magnitude refers to the dimensionless measure of the brightness of an object in a given waveband. A lower magnitude object is brighter than a higher magnitude one. A change in the magnitude by one implies a difference in brightness by a factor of 2.51, i.e. a magnitude 6 star is 2.51 times brighter than a magnitude 5 star. The Sun has a magnitude of -26, while Sirius, the brightest star in the night sky has a magnitude of -1.5. The faintest stars visible to human eye can be as dim as magnitude 6. Since the brightness changes with the wavelength of light, always notice the waveband in which the magnitude is mentioned[3].

More precisely, the '*apparent*' magnitude is defined as, $m_a = -2.5 \log\left(\frac{F_a}{F_0}\right)$, where F is the measured flux of the object in waveband a, and F_0 is the reference flux in the same waveband. The physical quantity that the magnitude measures is the **radiant flux**, i.e. the amount of radiation received by a given area on earth in a given time frame.

The apparent brightness of an object depends upon its intrinsic (true) brightness and its distance from the observer. This is

---

[3] *The examples stated here quote magnitudes in yellow light ($\lambda \sim 5800$ Å).*

quantified via '*absolute magnitude*' defined as,
$M = m - 5 (\log d_{pc} + 1)$, where d_{pc} is the distance of the object measured in parsec (pc).

For any astronomical object, the quantity '*colour*' therefore refers to the difference in the magnitude of an object measured through two different filters, e.g. *g* and *r*.

For stars, the colour index represents the surface temperature, such that lower value of colour implies bluer colour and hotter temperature. For a galaxy, the colour represents the mean age of the dominant stellar population in the galaxy. In other words, a blue galaxy tends to host younger stellar populations relative to its red counterparts.

The *colour-magnitude plot* is a powerful diagnostic to distinguish between the state of evolution of different types of galaxies (Figure 4). For instance, the 'sequence' of galaxies formed by old cluster galaxies is called the red sequence, while the congregation of young, blue galaxies observed in the region mapped by blue colours and lower luminosities is referred to as the 'blue cloud'. The sparsely populated region of the plot in between these two is called the 'green valley'. The galaxies in the green valley are believed to be transiting from the blue cloud to the red sequence (or vice-versa).

TOPCAT: For the following (and some of the other exercises in this book) we will make use of the software TOPCAT, which is a java based analysis software tool. It can be downloaded from http://www.star.bris.ac.uk/~mbt/topcat/. Even the lighter web version of TOPCAT[4] will suffice for these exercises. TOPCAT is a very easy to use, user-friendly software. It is also more powerful (especially for large datasets) in comparison to its competitors.

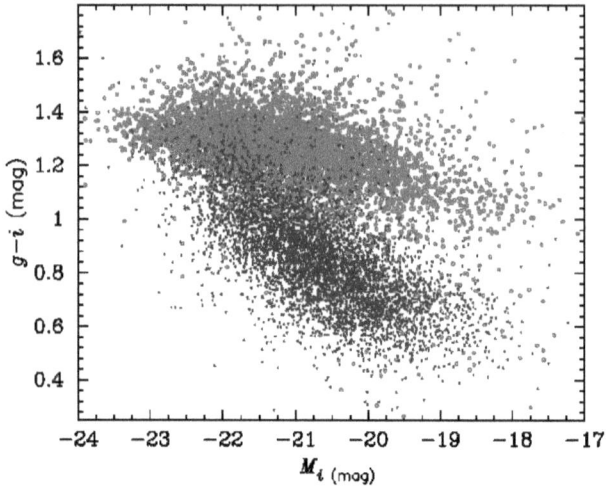

Figure 4: The colour magnitude plot of galaxies showing the 'red sequence' of old, elliptical galaxies (big points), and the 'blue cloud' of young, star-forming galaxies (dots). Do notice that there is a considerable overlap between the two populations as well, suggesting colour is an important, but insufficient factor for determining the properties of galaxies.

Exercise: Let us now learn about the classification of galaxies by plotting a 'colour-magnitude' diagram using TOPCAT, and photometric data from the SDSS. An example is shown in Figure 4. Table 6 lists mean wavelength for the five SDSS filters.

---

[4] *You may use any other traditional software packages such as MS EXCEL etc. for these exercises, although trying out TOPCAT is highly recommended.*

The data to be used for this exercise is provided in a CSV file at https://tinyurl.com/colourmag. These data were taken from the *NASA-Sloan Atlas*[5] (N-S Atlas, henceforth), and the morphological classification from the citizen science project *Galaxy Zoo*[6].

Table 6: Filters used by the Sloan Digital Sky Survey	
Filter	**Wavelength (Å)**
u (ultraviolet)	3543
g (green)	4770
r (red)	6231
i (near infrared)	7625
z (infrared)	9134

The CSV file contains the position information, a colour (called 'gminusi', $g - i$), absolute magnitude ('absmagi', M_i), as well as an indicator of morphology for each galaxy. Note that the morphological type is identified by having a flag set to '1' if the galaxy was classified as 'spiral', 'elliptical' or 'uncertain' in the respective columns.

You will notice that a large fraction of the galaxies in this dataset are classified as 'uncertain'. This is because the SDSS images are shallow images of !~ 55 seconds exposure. Although this is enough exposure for imaging large and/or nearby galaxies, it is insufficient to capture the details in the structure of faint and/or small galaxies. In case of latter, higher exposure time as well as

[5] *http://www.nsatlas.org/*

[6] *https://www.zooniverse.org/projects/zookeeper/galaxy-zoo/*

images with better resolution[7] are the only way to observe the fine features.

- First, using the N-S Atlas magnitudes, make a colour-magnitude diagram using the absolute magnitude and colour. (Hint: You may have to zoom into regions with higher galaxy density by changing the axis range to get a better idea.)
What do you notice about the distribution of galaxies?

- In TOPCAT it is possible to visualise the galaxies in each column. To do so, after loading the CSV file in TOPCAT, click on the icon with a lightening symbol on it in the top panel (Hint: hovering your pointer over the icons in the top panel provides a brief description of their intended use. The description of this one reads 'Display actions invoked when rows are selected'). This will open the 'Activation actions' window. In the left hand side panel of this window, select 'Display cutout image'. The option 'Use Sky coordinates in TOPCAT' should already be selected. On the right hand side, ensure that the relevant position columns are selected for the coordinates. Click on the 'Display cutout image' tab. In the 'cutout service' option select SDSS colour images, and in dimensions 150. Close this window. Open the CSV table by double clicking on the file name in the main TOPCAT panel. Now, selecting any row in this table will display an SDSS image of the galaxy in a separate 'image'

---

[7] *Recall the Rayleigh criterion, according to which resolution, $\theta = \lambda/D$, where D is the diameter of the optical lens (or mirror), i.e., the larger is the lens (or mirror), lower will be the resolution of the observed object at fixed λ. This is one of the governing principles behind the quest to create large mirror telescopes, such as the 30 metre diameter mirror for the Thirty Meter Telescope (TMT).*

window[8].
You fill find that all the galaxies in this dataset are viewed almost face-on. Why does that make things simpler for this exercise?

- Why do we call the difference between the magnitude measured in the SDSS-g and i band a 'colour'?

- Next, let's add the information about morphology from the Galaxy Zoo. Use the 'column statistics' capability of TOPCAT to quickly figure out the fraction of galaxies which are classified as ellipticals? As spirals? As uncertain?
Alternatively, create 'subsets' by selecting the 'display row subset' icon from the top panel. 'Define a new subset', for instance, by choosing all rows with 'spiral==1'. Lets call this subset as spirals. In the 'row subsets' window you will see the size of this subset. Similarly, create other subsets for ellipticals and uncertain galaxies.

- We are now ready to plot the colour-magnitude diagram with different morphological classes. Select the 'plane plotting window' from the top panel and plot the colour-magnitude diagram. To check the distribution of individual morphological classes, select the file name in the LHS of the plot control window and click on the 'subsets' tab. This allows you to select individual subsets to be included in the plot. The 'form' tab allows for changing the symbol colour, sizes etc. for clarity in the plots.
Superpose the spirals on the ellipticals *(be sure to do it in that order)* using different symbols/colours. Check out their distributions separately by checking/unchecking the subset name. What can you conclude?

---

[8] *Image loading time depends upon the chosen image size and the internet speed.*

STAR CLUSTERS

When a gas cloud collapses to form stars, many stars of different masses are often born together. All these stars having an almost identical chemical composition, are together called a 'star cluster'. Although they might differ from each other in terms of magnetic field, rotation properties and membership of binaries etc., their evolution is determined solely by their initial mass[9].

Figure 5: (left:) *The Pleiades open cluster (Image source: DSS), and (right:) globular cluster NGC 6229 (Image source: SDSS).*

---

[9] *The term 'initial mass' specifically implies the mass of a star at which it begins to burn hydrogen to attain hydrostatic equilibrium. Once this happens, a 'protostar' becomes a star. The mass of a star keeps changing throughout its lifetime.*

Star clusters can primarily be sub-classified into two categories:

- *Globular clusters:* These are old clusters which formed when our galaxy was very young. They are very massive, red and contain more than 10,000 stars. On average, globular clusters are found to be older than 11 billion years, and have little to no gas and dust. They are 20-100 pc across. Globular clusters are found in the halo of the galaxy, surrounding the galaxy disk.

- *Open clusters:* They are smaller (< 10 pc across) and bluer than the globular clusters, and comprise a few hundreds to few thousand stars. These are relatively younger clusters not older than 10 billion years, and hence may contain dust and gas.

Since high mass (i.e. more luminous) stars have a shorter life span than their lower mass counterparts, older clusters naturally have more and more low mass, cooler stars. Therefore, by studying which stars have evolved off the main sequence[10] astronomers can estimate the age of a star cluster.

Exercise: Lists of open and globular clusters observed by the SDSS are given at https://tinyurl.com/open-clusters and https://tinyurl.com/globular-clusters, link respectively.

- Choose any one star cluster of each category.

- Go to http://skyserver.sdss.org/dr16/en/tools/chart/navi.aspx and enter the name of the chosen star cluster. Hit 'resolve'. This will show you a multi-colour image of the star cluster.

---

[10] *Main sequence is the relation between luminosity and temperature of a star, such that high luminosity stars are hotter and fainter stars are cooler.*

- Check the 'Photometric objects' box in the 'Drawing options' to highlight all objects in the image for which photometric data are available. Clicking on any of these objects will show their data on the top right corner of the image. Note down the g and r band magnitudes for as many stars as possible, using your wisdom to decide whether they belong to the cluster[11].

- Populate the r vs $g - r$ colour-magnitude plot for both star clusters. (Preferably on the same plot with different symbols and colours, or separately but using the same range for both axes for comparison.)

- Note your observations. What differences (if any) do you observe? Why? Are all your chosen stars part of the cluster? Try to justify your findings.

Tip: (i) Choose star clusters wisely. The ones with very bright central stars or very crowded field will not have photometry available for many stars.

(ii) More information about your chosen star clusters (or any documented astronomical object) can be obtained from https://ned.ipac.caltech.edu/forms/byname.html.

---

[11] Choose wisely! Remember stars are point-like objects, so do not include any extended sources in your list. Globular clusters will contain yellowish-red and red stars, while open clusters will have blue ones. Be careful though because occasionally some high redshift galaxies may be classified as 'stars' by the SDSS algorithm ad vice-versa. Will you be able to spot them in the colour-magnitude plot?

SHAPES OF GALAXIES

On the basis of shape (or *morphology,* as the astronomers like to say!), galaxies can primarily be classified into spirals and ellipticals. As the name suggests, the latter are elliptical in shape and appear red when observed in visible light (~3000-9000 Å). The spiral galaxies on the other hand, are blue in colour due to the presence of young stellar populations in them. This also means that the spiral galaxies have younger mean age, and they are forming more stars relative to their elliptical counterparts. Consequently, elliptical galaxies are often termed as 'dead and red'.

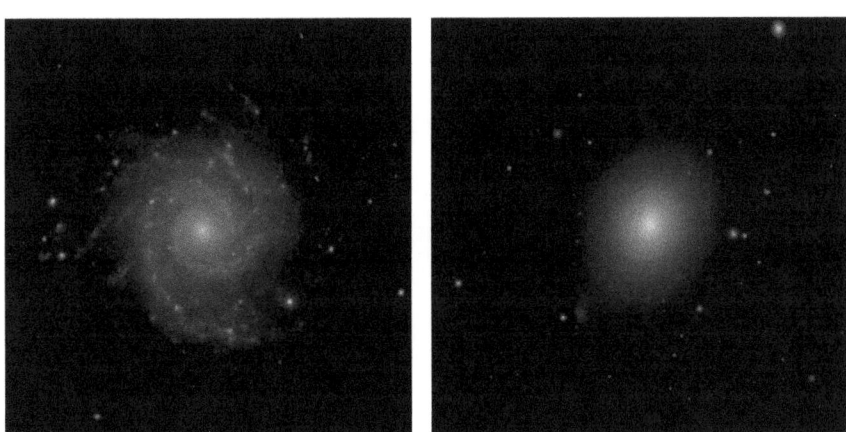

<u>Figure 6</u>: *A typical spiral (left) and elliptical (right) galaxy. (Image source: SDSS)*

Exercise 1: Enter the field identifiers listed in Table 7 on http://skyserver.sdss.org/dr14/en/tools/getimg/fields.aspx and identify the morphological types of galaxies.

Table 7: SDSS fields for identifying galaxy morphology.		
Run	Camcol	Field
752	1	244
2662	4	243
752	1	331
1737	6	11
756	4	198
2738	2	196
752	1	432
3325	3	319
3325	2	216
3325	2	215
3325	3	230 (two galaxies)
2738	3	122 (two galaxies)
3325	3	352
3325	1	356
3325	1	359

Exercise 2: Go to http://skyserver.sdss.org/dr14/en/tools/chart/navi.aspx to access the SDSS 'navigate' tool. Enter 'Abell 1656' in the name resolver on the left hand side of the page to get an image

of the famous Coma (Abell 1656) cluster (!~ 100 Mpc). Coma is one of the richest clusters in the nearby universe. Click on a few galaxies therein[12] and note down their u, g, r magnitudes. The information on individual galaxies can be saved by selecting the galaxy and then clicking on 'add to notes' from the right hand side panel. Once done, 'show notes' will show the data for all the saved galaxies and can be downloaded by the user.

Plot these on the $u - g$ versus $g - r$ colour-colour diagram.

(i) Can you deduce anything about the nature of cluster galaxies from this colour-colour plot?

(ii) Can you spot galaxies which are obviously not part of the cluster? (Note: This information can be checked for galaxies with spectra using the redshift information.)

---

[12] *Remember the orange coloured elliptical galaxies are more likely to be members of the cluster.*

LIGHT PROFILE OF GALAXIES

In the early twentieth century, when images for a few thousand nearby galaxies were available, astronomers could visually classify them all. However, with the advent of technology, we now have images for billions of galaxies, going very far back in time, in multiple filters. So far, the Sloan Digital Sky survey (SDSS) alone has observed half a billion unique objects in five broadband filters (*ugriz*). The exponential increase in the availability of data therefore requires computation driven automated techniques, which, aided by human wisdom are used to create meaningful datasets to study evolution of galaxies.

In this chapter we will learn about one such method of decoding the shape of a galaxy using a quantitative measure of galaxy's morphology. This method involves the 'light profile' of a galaxy. In simple terms, if we imagine a galaxy to be divided into a set of concentric circles, 'light profile' is the distribution of flux averaged over each annulus in the image of the galaxy, plotted as a function of the mean radius of the annulus.

Analysis of a light profile can reveal interesting facts about the physical properties of a galaxy even without looking at its image. Furthermore, parameters derived from the light profile can be used as quantitative measures of galaxy's morphology, therefore making it possible to compare, and statistically analyse a large sample of galaxies in less time.

Exercise 1: We are now ready to create the light profile for our first galaxy. Let us do this for the nearby spiral galaxy Messier 33 (M33)[13].

- Download the image analysis software DS9 from http://ds9.si.edu/site/Home.html. DS9 is a very powerful, yet easy to use image analysis software available to be used for all operating systems.

- Open a new DS9 window, and proceed to Analysis > Image servers > DSS (SAO). The DS9 capability allows the user to access the images of the sky from the digital sky survey (DSS) database (and many others) via the internet. Type 'M33' in the object field, and change the width and height of the image to be downloaded to at least 60 arcminutes, since M33 is a big nearby galaxy. 'Retrieve' the image of the M33 galaxy from the selected server.

- Once the image is loaded, go to Edit > Regions to enable overlaying regions on the image. Now go to Regions > Shape > Annulus. This will overplot two circles on the image and open a new control window.

---

[13] *Charles Messier (1730-1817) was a French astronomers who discovered several comets. While he was searching for transient celestial objects, he happened to study many other objects as well. Messier published a catalogue of 110 objects, all of which appeared similar through his basic telescope. But we now know that his catalogue is a mixed bag of objects including supernovae, planetary nebulae, star clusters and galaxies. These are popularly called the messier objects and designated by their M number.*

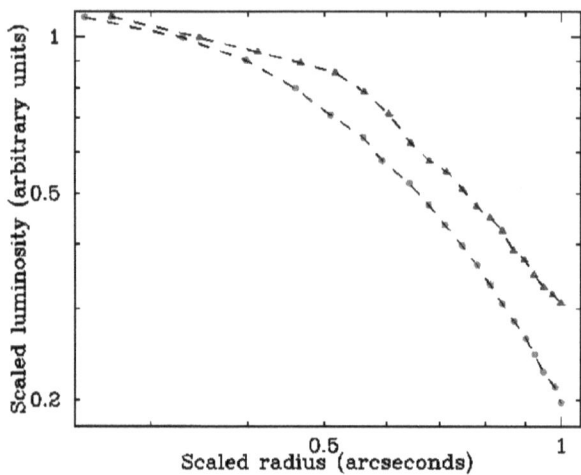

Figure 7: The DSS images of a typical elliptical (left) and spiral (right) galaxy (M31 and M33, respectively).

- In the control window choose the number of annulus and their attributes such as spacing between annuli, colour, width etc.. Each annulus can also be moved individually to a selected size.

- Once you are satisfied with the placement of the annuli, click on the Annulus control window (to activate it), and then go to Analysis > Radial profile. This will plot a radial profile of your galaxy. You might want to change the axes of the plot to log-log, in order to replicate Figure 8.

- Now, go to Analysis > Statistics to access the data shown in your plot.

Figure 7 shows the images, and Figure 8 shows the light profiles of the galaxies M31 (elliptical) and M33 (spiral) using the data obtained using the above exercise for *Digitized sky survey (DSS)*[14]

---

[14] *https://archive.eso.org/dss/dss*

images. Since the two galaxies have different angular sizes, both the axes are scaled such that the maximum radius and flux are 1. Can you spot any obvious differences in the two profiles?

Note how smoothly the profile for the elliptical galaxy declines. In fact, the light profile for elliptical galaxies of different luminosities (and hence masses) has been successfully fitted using the mathematical function $I(r) = I_b(0) \exp{-7.669[(\frac{r}{r_e})^{1/4}]}$, where $I_b(0)$ is the intensity at radius r_e. This is known as the *de Vaucouleurs' profile*. The generalised version of this function is the *Sérsic profile* given as $I(r) = I_b(0) \exp[-b_n(r/r_e)^{1/n}]$. The parameters of these models are central intensity $I_b(0)$, effective radius r_e, and Sérsic index n. The quantity b_n is defined such that r_e encloses half of the total luminosity of the galaxy. As can be seen from these equations, $n \approx 4$ for a perfect elliptical profile.

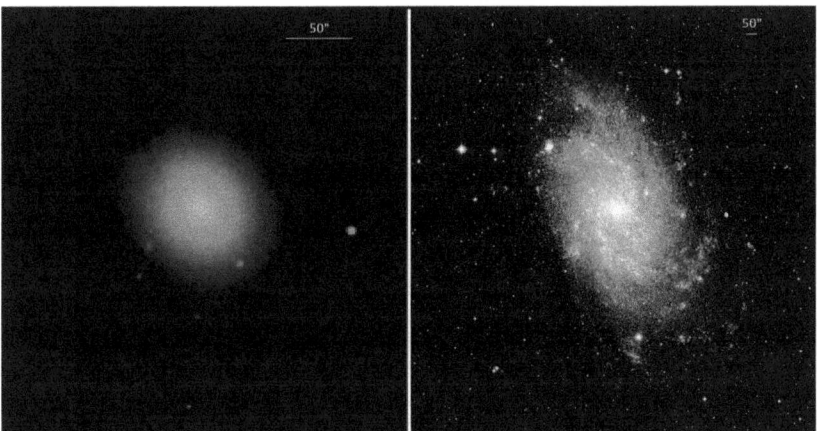

Figure 8: A comparison between radial light profiles of M31 (dots) and M33 (triangles) is shown in a log-log plane. The differences in the profiles directly correlate with the difference in the appearance of the two galaxies (see text)

The profile for the spiral galaxy can be split into at least two components: an exponentially declining curve upto scaled radius $! \lesssim 0.4$, and then an almost linear decline in flux. This distinction is due to the central 'bulge' and the outer 'disk' components of a spiral galaxy. In many aspects, the central bulge can be considered a scaled-down version of an elliptical galaxy. Also notice the small bumps in this profile. These correspond to the bright star-forming regions embedded in the spiral arms of the galaxy. The Sérsic index for a perfect exponential disk is 1.

The advent of technology has made it possible to capture very high resolution images of nearby galaxies. Consequently, it has now become possible to resolve an additional component, the 'nucleus' at the heart of a spiral galaxy. The nucleus may be modelled separately than the other two components.

Exercise 2: Once you are comfortable with the 'annulus' function discussed in exercise 1, try using the 'elliptical annulus' which is a more appropriate representation of the shape of most galaxies. Do you spot any differences in the profiles with the two different sets of annuli: circular and elliptical?

Exercise 3: Try to get the radial profiles for galaxies with different morphologies, e.g. an elliptical (such as M31) and a spiral (M33). Copy the data for the radial profiles in a separate text file, and plot them together (using different colours) on the same plot as shown in Figure 8.
Can you interpret the obvious structural differences using these 1-d light profiles alone? Try other galaxies, spirals with different

position angles[15] etc., and try to deduce your findings based on the light profiles.

Exercise 4 (advanced): Write a small program in your favourite coding language to fit a Sérsic profile to any galaxy of your choice. What is the Sérsic index? Does it matches your expectation based on the image of the galaxy?

---

[15] *Position angle indicates the 'tilt' of the galaxy relative to the plane of the sky. A face-on spiral will have all its spiral arms clearly visible, where as an edge-on galaxy will only appear as a bar with thickness equivalent to the thickness of the galaxy's disk.*

MEASURING REDSHIFT OF GALAXIES

The spectrum of a galaxy is more complex than a star because it is an aggregate of many different stellar populations comprising the galaxy. However, we can still use it to find the distance to a galaxy by studying the shift in the spectral lines relative to their rest frame wavelength. This method works on the same principle as that of the Doppler effect, i.e. a source of light receding from the observer stretches the electromagnetic waves towards the red end of the spectrum. As a consequence, the lines in the spectrum will shift towards the longer wavelength relative to the wavelength in the frame of rest.

The first significant extragalactic redshift was measured for the Andromeda galaxy (M31) by Vesto Slipher in 1912. In 1920s Edwin Hubble used the 100-inch telescope at the Mt. Wilson observatory to measure redshifts of a few tens of galaxies. By combining his measurements with Slipher's, he concluded what is now famously called the Hubble's law (discussed in the next chapter).

Specifically, The redshift (or blueshift) of a galaxy is the shifting of its spectral features to longer (or shorter) wavelengths primarily due to the combination of Doppler motions and the general expansion of the Universe. In literature, often the term 'radial velocity' is primarily used for Doppler motions caused by gravitational interactions, while 'redshift' is reserved for the cosmological effects. It is however, generally not possible to separate out cosmological expansion and Doppler velocities except for very nearby galaxies, and galaxies known to be members of clusters.

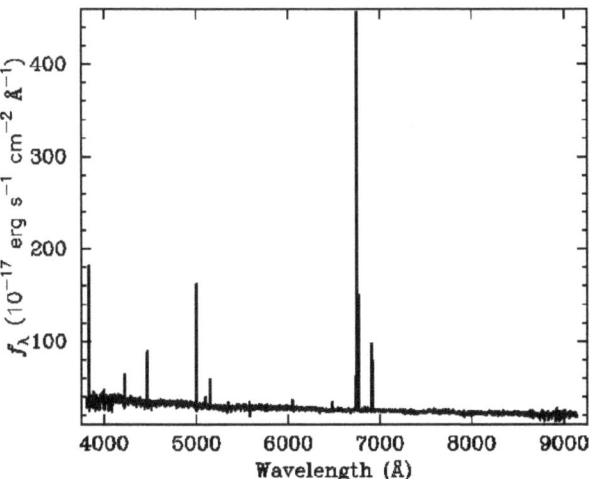

Figure 9: Typical spectrum of a star-forming galaxy. Compare the common features of this spectrum with the stellar spectra shown in Figure 3. Can you spot any differences? (data source: SDSS)

In terms of wavelength, redshift z, is defined as
$$z = \frac{\lambda_o - \lambda_e}{\lambda_e} \text{ i.e., } \lambda_o = (1+z)\lambda_e,$$
where the subscripts 0 and e refer to the wavelength of the observed and emitted radiation, respectively. In the frequency domain, redshift is defined as

$$z = \frac{\nu_e - \nu_o}{\nu_o} = \frac{\nu_e}{\nu_o} - 1.$$ The difference between these formulae is due to the fact that wavelength increases, but frequency decreases with increasing redshift.

The shift in the spectral lines can be interpreted as the radial velocity of the source with respect to the observer, or, its escape velocity caused due to the general expansion of space. While the former is true for nearby objects such as stars within our own galaxy, the latter is applicable for more distant sources. In most cases however, it is nearly impossible to distinguish between these two interpretations, because a galaxy (i) has physical motions called 'peculiar velocities' due to gravitational interactions with the surrounding objects, (ii) moves away from the observer due to the cosmic expansion, and (iii) may have some other motion relative to the observer. Therefore, as a general rule, at $z \gg 1$, the Doppler shift is assumed to be completely dominated by cosmological expansion.

Exercise: Let us make use of the spectroscopic data provided by the SDSS to measure redshifts for some galaxies.

- Go to https://dr14.sdss.org/optical/spectrum/view and access the spectra using the information provided in Table 8.

- The observed spectrum is plotted along with a model spectrum (often shown in red) which is used to measure the redshift of the galaxy by the SDSS pipeline. It is possible to zoom into the spectrum simply by selecting a rectangular region on it. Double clicking on the spectrum will show the full spectrum again.

- Zoom into the regions of a few strong spectral lines such as Hα, Hβ, [NII] etc.. Although we can measure redshift using a single spectral line, it is often advisable to average over more than one lines to reduce uncertainties. (Hint: Choose spectral lines with good model fit for better estimation.)

- Now compare the observed redshift (λ_o) with its known rest-frame value[16].

- The redshift can be calculated using the formula $z = \dfrac{\lambda_o}{\lambda_e} - 1$.

Compare this value to the one estimated by the SDSS pipeline. How close did you get? Does averaging over more than one spectral lines improve your estimate?

Table 8: Plate, MJD, fiber ID for spectra of galaxies.	
Plate/MJD	**Fiber ID**
268/51633	562
266/51602	562

---

[16] Some spectral lines used by the SDSS are listed at https://classic.sdss.org/dr6/algorithms/linestable.html .

THE HUBBLE LAW

The radial velocity of galaxies measured using the Doppler shift of spectral lines is almost always positive, implying that all of these galaxies are moving away from us. In 1928, Edwin Hubble discovered that the recessional velocity of galaxies increases with their distance from us. Therefore, he proposed a linear relationship between the radial velocity v and the distance D of the galaxy, which came to be known as the *Hubble law*, $v = H_0 D$, where H_0 is called the *Hubble's constant*.

Following Hubble's footsteps, when we plot the radial velocity of a sample of galaxies as a function of their distance, the resulting distribution is approximated by a straight line whose slope is determined by the constant H_0. The fact that almost all galaxies are moving away with a velocity which increases linearly with their distance from us, is inferred as an evidence that the Universe itself is expanding. The rate of expansion H_0, as determined from data in the last few decades is found to be !$\sim 65 - 80$ km/s/Mpc.

Exercise 1: For this exercise we will once again make use of TOPCAT.

- Create a simple text file using the data provided in Table 9. Alternatively, a larger version of this table can be accessed at https://tinyurl.com/hubbledist in ASCII format.

- Load these data into TOPCAT. For this exercise we will use the distance and the redshift columns only. Note that these distances are redshift-independent, i.e. they are measured using methods other than Doppler redshift. Some of these galaxies also have spectra available, so we can use these data to test the Hubble's law and measure the Hubble's constant.

- Create a new column by right clicking at the top of any column name > create new synthetic column. Call this column "velocity" with value as 300,000 times the redshift. This will convert the redshift to a radial velocity[17] in units of km/s, assuming velocity of light, $c = 300,000$ km/s and the fact that for small redshift $v \approx cz$.

- Use the plotting tool (plane plot) to plot D (Mpc) vs velocity (km/s).

- In the plot control window select Form > Linear fit, in order to fit a straight line through the data[18] and note the value of m, the slope of the fitted line. This is the value of the Hubble constant H_0 for these data in units of km/s/Mpc.

---

[17] Note that this approximation is valid only for $z \ll 1$.

[18] There are many statistical methods to do this. Topcat uses the least square method to fit a straight line to two-dimensional data.

Table 9: Distances and redshifts for some galaxies

Galaxy	m-M	Error	D (Mpc)	Redshift
M096	29.95	0.02	9.74	0.00299
NGC 6951	31.61	0.04	20.9	0.00475
NGC 7329	33.68	0.02	53.7	0.01085
NGC 4493	34.93	0.03	94.6	0.02316
SN 2010gn	35.82	0.04	141	0.0312
SN 1992ae	37.88	0.03	351	0.075
UGC 10030	35.46	0.04	120	0.02986
[M96b] J152109.75 + 275508	39.14	0.02	596	0.13
SDSS J100128.71 + 015147.1	40.05	0.03	863	0.184
[NSB2006] J022618.47 - 041843.2	40.57	0.03	1070	0.211
[HSP2005] J141635.93 + 522844.20	41.26	0.01	1340	0.337
LSSP J142053.55 + 523620.4	41.87	0.03	1630	0.449
2003fp	42.13	0.03	1840	0.449
SNLS 05D3jq	42.42	0.04	1930	0.58
SNLS 06D3et	42.79	0.04	2300	0.576
[HSP2005] J142206.87 + 521343.46	43.11	0.04	2690	0.552
[AGR2006] J142232.61 + 523849.3	43.21	0.03	3020	0.451

Table 9: Distances and redshifts for some galaxies

Galaxy	m-M	Error	D (Mpc)	Redshift
SCP 06H03	43.59	0.04	2830	0.85
[SRG2009] 04126	43.86	0.03	2980	0.98

Exercise 2: In this exercise you are expected to measure the redshift of galaxies of your choice, and use them to plot the Hubble diagram.

- Access the Sloan Digital Sky Survey (SDSS) website http://skyserver.sdss.org/dr14/en/tools/chart/navi.aspx.

- Type the common name of galaxies in the left tab called 'name' and resolve to get the information about that galaxy. If it has been observed by the SDSS, a postage stamp of the spectra will appear in the bottom right corner next to the image of the galaxy. (To begin, choose some targets like UGC 10030, NGC 6951 etc. from Table 9.)

- Click on the spectra to see its enlarged version. Notice that the marked emission lines are shifted from their rest frame wavelength. For instance, the rest frame wavelength for the Hα line is 6562.08 Å (λ_0)[19]. Note the shifted wavelength (λ_e). The redshift of the galaxy is given as $(\lambda_e - \lambda_0)/\lambda_0$. Check the obtained value against the redshift quoted on the spectrum. How close did you get?

---

[19] *Some spectral lines used by the SDSS survey are listed on https://classic.sdss.org/dr6/algorithms/linestable.html .*

- Use the obtained redshift with the redshift-independent distances from Table 9 (column 4) to plot the Hubble diagram.

MASS OF A CLUSTER

Observations have revealed that a substantial fraction (!~ 40 %) of all galaxies are found in groups and clusters. Clusters of galaxies are the largest gravitationally bound structures in the Universe. The cluster environment offers a higher galaxy density, as well as hot intra-cluster gas to the existing and incoming galaxy members. This gas in clusters is known as the *intra-cluster medium (ICM)*. As a consequence, galaxies in clusters are likely to evolve more quickly by interacting with each other, as well as the hot ICM.

Figure 10: The brightest cluster galaxy (NGC 4889) surrounded by other members at the centre of the Coma cluster (z=0.023). (Image source: SDSS).

Even though the idea had been in existence for a while, the first strong evidence of the existence of dark matter was presented in the year 1933. Fritz Zwicky used the Mount Wilson observatory to measure the light, and consequently the mass of visible matter in a cluster of galaxies. Zwicky discovered that the cluster was much more massive than the luminous matter present in it. Based on the results, he concluded that there is some other 'dunkle materie' i.e. dark matter (in German) which is keeping everything together in the cluster. The dark matter it seems, attracts due to gravity, just like luminous matter.

Later, studies of rotational speeds of individual galaxies also revealed the presence of dark matter. To this date, many other observations point towards the existence of dark matter. In fact, it is now well known that dark matter is around five times more abundant than luminous matter in the universe.

In this chapter we will use the data for the Coma cluster to discover dark matter just like Zwicky. But prior to that we need to review an important theoretical principle— the Virial theorem.

The *Virial theorem* states that, for a gravitationally bound system in equilibrium, the total (time-averaged) energy is always half of the potential energy (time-averaged). i.e.,

$$2T + U = 0 \qquad (1)$$

In an astronomical context, one can use this very simple, but very powerful result by making two simple assumptions:

(i) the kinetic energy of the constituent particles in the system, $T = Mv^2/2$, where M is the total mass and v is the mean velocity of particles (aka stars in a galaxy, or galaxies in a cluster depending upon the context), and,

(ii) the gravitational potential energy of the system, $U = GM^2/R$, where G is the gravitational constant and R is the effective radius (size) of the system. Under these assumptions, the Virial equation can be re-written as,

$$M = v^2 R/G \qquad (2)$$

So essentially, the viral theorem helps us relate an unobservable but fundamental property of the system, to two quantities which can be determined empirically.

Exercise: For this exercise we will use the table dm.txt[20] which can be accessed at https://tinyurl.com/clusmass. The columns are: i. galaxy ID, ii. x position of the galaxy measured northward relative to the cluster's centre (in arcseconds), iii, y position of the galaxy measured westward relative to the cluster's centre (in arcseconds), iv. b-band magnitude, v. b-r colour, vi. heliocentric radial velocity in km/s, vii. Error in vi., and, viii. quality of redshift ranging from 1 (best) to 3 where available.

Watch out for outliers, i.e. galaxies which appear in the same direction as the Coma Cluster, but are either much closer to us, or much farther away than the cluster along the same line of sight. These outliers can be identified by their very different values of radial velocity relative to the cluster's mean redshift. Based on these data, let us try to answer some fundamental questions about the Coma cluster.

- What is the systemic radial velocity of the Coma cluster?

---

[20] *This table is sourced from Biviano et al., A&AS, 111, 265, 1995; http://vizier.cfa.harvard.edu/viz-bin/VizieR-3?-source=J/A%2bAS/111/265/table2*

- What is the radial velocity dispersion of the Coma cluster? (This is part of the left hand side of the Virial equation.)

- Assuming the distance to the Coma Cluster to be 100 Mpc ($z = 0.023$), calculate the typical distance (in parsecs) of the member galaxies from the centre of the cluster?
  In order to do so, use the angular distance of each galaxy from the centre of the cluster, west and north, respectively, as given in the data table (in units of arcseconds).

- Now use equation (2) to estimate the mass of the Coma Cluster. Express your result in $M_\odot$, for ease of comparison with the literature.

- Following Zwicky, assume Coma cluster contains 1000 galaxies, each having an average luminosity of !~ $8.5 \times 10^7\ L_\odot$. Use this information to compute the average mass per galaxy, and then the total mass of the cluster. How does that compare to the mass estimated using the Virial theorem in the previous step?

Note: Zwicky's estimate of the distance to the cluster was significantly smaller than our current value, so his calculation of the mass of the cluster was also significantly smaller. But he noticed a troubling discrepancy in the ratio between the mass of this cluster and the amount of light emitted by its galaxies, and, since that ratio is independent of distance, the puzzle remains to this day. Zwicky argued that since the mass-to-light ratio for galaxies is off by two orders of magnitude, there must be a "dark" component of matter, of which, most of the galaxies are formed.

MASS OF A GALAXY

A galaxy is an amalgamation of stars, dust, gas and dark matter bound together by gravity. The stars, dust and gas collectively comprise the *'baryonic mass'*[21] of a galaxy. For most galaxies, stars form the bulk of their baryonic mass.

When compared to their dark counterpart, the 'luminous' components of a galaxy can be investigated observationally through the emitted radiation. But a galaxy's total mass may also include a sizeable amount of dark matter, which is thought to be composed of non-baryonic particles such as neutrinos. To measure the dark matter mass of a galaxy indirect techniques are employed, one of which is the subject of this chapter.

Observations show that the luminosity of stars (L) is related to their mass (M), such that $L \equiv L_\odot(M/M_\odot)$, where the subscript ☉ implies that both luminosity and mass are measured in solar units. This implies that if we could measure the radiation emitted by a galaxy across all wavelengths (i.e. the total luminosity), we can estimate its baryonic mass. The *mass-to-light ratio, M/L*, can therefore be used as an indirect measure of the fractional

---

[21] *Heavy subatomic particles such as protons and neutrons are called baryons.*

contribution of dark matter to the total mass of the galaxy[22]. In other words, if a galaxy is found to be more massive than the mass expected from the luminosity of stars and gas, it must contain dark matter.

In order to measure the total mass of a galaxy independent of luminosity, one can measure its dynamical mass. The dynamical mass of galaxies can be measured directly from their 'rotation curve'. A *rotation curve* is a plot showing the distribution of the radial speed of the observed stars and gas in a galaxy as a function of their distance from the centre as shown in Figure 11.

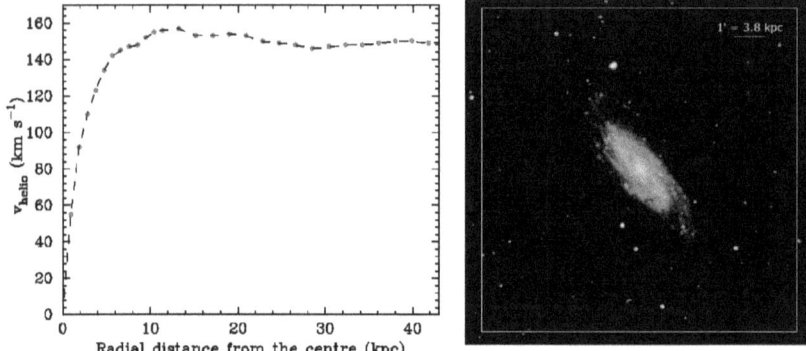

Figure 11: (left:) *The rotation curve of galaxy NGC 3198 shows the characteristic flattening representative of the presence of dark matter in the galaxy*[23]. *(right:) Optical image of NGC 3198. The white box shows the same region as represented by the rotation curve. (Image source: DSS)*

---

[22] *Although the discussion here is in the context of galaxies, the same principle applies to larger objects such as clusters of galaxies, and smaller entities, such as star clusters.*

[23] *This rotation curve is based on data provided by van Albada et al., ApJ, 295, 305, 1985.*

The circular velocity v_{circ} is the velocity that a star must have in order to maintain its circular orbit at a particular distance from the centre of the galaxy[24]. For a disk galaxy, the circular velocity is the orbital velocity of stars moving in the plane of the galaxy. So, the absolute value of acceleration $g = v_{circ}^2/R$ (assuming circular symmetry).

Furthermore, under the assumption of spherical symmetry for a disk galaxy, the gravitational acceleration at a distance R from the centre of the galaxy is given as $GM(R)/R^2$, where $M(R)$ is the mass enclosed within the radius R. Therefore, $\frac{v_{circ}^2}{R} = \frac{GM(R)}{R^2}$, and hence $v_{circ} = \sqrt{\frac{GM(R)}{R}}$. This implies, that if we can evaluate v_{circ} at different radii, then we can estimate the distribution of mass as a function of R as, $M(R) = \frac{v_{circ}^2 R}{G}$.

This result suggests that the circular velocity, $v_{circ} \propto \sqrt{M(R)/R}$ should decline with radius beyond the disk scale length[25]. But as evidently seen in Figure 11, this is not the case, thereby implying the presence of invisible matter in galaxies.

---

[24] *This assumes that the galaxy has a symmetric potential around the centre, although this is not true for disk galaxies.*

[25] *The scale length is the radius at which the luminosity of the disk drops by a factor of e (~ 2.17) relative to the centre of the galaxy. The disk scale length of NGC 3198 = 2.68 kpc (Figure 11; van Albada et al., 1985).*

Exercise: Let us now test the contribution of dark matter to the mass of the spiral galaxy NGC 4701[26]. In order to do so:

- Find the *g* and *r*-band magnitudes of NGC 4701 using SDSS DR 14 website http://skyserver.sdss.org/dr14/en/tools/chart/navi.aspx. Using these magnitudes, find the colour (*g* − *r*).

- Convert the *(g − r)* colour to *(B − V)* colour using the conversion relation given in Table 1 of Jester et al. (2005) as mentioned here http://www.sdss3.org/dr10/algorithms/sdssUBVRITransform.php#Jester2005.

- Now determine the mass-to-luminosity ratio in the *K*-band (M/L_K) by using the closed box model of Bell & de Jong (http://iopscience.iop.org/article/10.1086/319728/fulltext/52546.text.html; use the relation given in Table 1).

- The NASA Extragalactic Database (NED) is a very useful repository for information on various astronomical objects. We will now access the NED website https://ned.ipac.caltech.edu/ to determine the 2MASS flux[1] (F_{K_s} in W m^{-2} Hz^{-1}) for NGC 4701. This can be done by 'searching' for NGC 4701. Once the data for this galaxy shows, click on 'photometry & SED'. You may notice multiple entries corresponding to the same filter. This is because NED shows all the different measurements performed by different authors without any biases. You may choose any of them.

- Use the 'Redshifts' tab in NED to determine the luminosity distance for NGC 4701. Now we can estimate the luminosity of NGC 4701 in the K_s-band by using the flux and distance in

---

[26] *This exercise is based on Das et al., ApJ, 871, 197, 2019 and personal interactions with Dr. Mousumi Das (IIA, Bengaluru).*

the standard relation $F = L/4\pi D^2$. Assume the bandwidth for this filter to be $\Delta\lambda = 0.262\mu m$.

- Using the M/L$_K$ determined earlier, evaluate the stellar mass of NGC 4701 (in M$_\odot$).

- NGC 4701 has a flat rotation curve of 110 km/s and disk radius of 160". Try to evaluate the dynamical mass of the galaxy (in M$_\odot$)? (Hint: Use the luminosity distance to find disk size in units of length).

- Can you now determine the relative percentage of dark matter in this galaxy? Summarise your interpretation of NGC 4701 based on the above results.

MORE RESOURCES ON THE INTERNET

Besides data, several free teaching resources are available on the web. The following list is not exhaustive, but shows how many resources are available to be explored.

S. No.	Website	Remarks
1	https://classic.sdss.org/education/	Resources for students and teachers of high school onwards. Images and spectra of billions of sources available instantaneously.
2	https://astro.unl.edu/	Teaching resources from the University of Nebraska-Lincoln. The native apps can be downloaded and run to demonstrate various astronomical phenomenon.

S. No.	Website	Remarks
3	http://www.pas.rochester.edu/~blackman/ast104/index0.html	Notes on various topics taught by Prof. Eric Blackman, University of Rochester.
4	https://www.zooniverse.org/projects/zookeeper/galaxy-zoo/	Citizen science project where you can contribute towards visual classification of objects.
5	http://ned.ipac.caltech.edu/level5/	A repository of review articles on various topics.
6	https://jila.colorado.edu/~pja/astr3730/index.html	Notes on various topics taught by Prof. Armitage, University of Colorado.
7	http://wittman.physics.ucdavis.edu/Animations/index.html	A collection of interesting animations for understanding astrophysical phenomenon hosted by Prof. David Wittman.
8	https://www.atnf.csiro.au/outreach/education/senior/astrophysics/index.html	Introduction to various topics by the Australia National Telescope Facility (ATNF).

SOLUTIONS

Most of the exercises in this book are designed such that learners will benefit from interactions with peers. Additional reading from standard textbooks will also be beneficial to answer the qualitative questions and clearing any doubts. In addition to that, explanation and answers to some of the quantitative questions are provided below.

1. Binary star systems

i. Assuming circular orbits, $v = (v_{max} + v_{min})/2$, where all velocities can be obtained from the velocity curve (use, $v = (\Delta\lambda/\lambda).c$, assuming $v \ll c$ where, c is the velocity of light). From the velocity curve, find out minimum and maximum velocities of the two stars (74.2 km s^{-1} and 150.0 km s^{-1}). $T = 1.92$ days.

ii. Put v_1, v_2, T in the formula for mass to get $M = 2.23\ M_\odot$. $\dfrac{m_1}{m_2} = \dfrac{v_2}{v_1} = 2.02$; so, $m_1 = 1.48\ M_\odot$, $m_2 = 0.74\ M_\odot$.

iii. On the MS $L \propto M^{3.5}$, so $L_1 \sim 4\ L_\odot$ and $L_2 \sim 0.35\ L_\odot$. Therefore, from the HRD star 1 is an F-type star and star 2 is a K-type star.

2. Colour

iv. An edge-on disk appears redder compared to its face-on version because the photons from the interior of the galaxy will have to pass through more material in the galaxy to reach the observer. This leads to 'reddening' because the photons are scattered and absorbed on the way, losing some of their energy and therefore shifting towards longer (lower-energy, redder) wavelength.

v. Historically, the difference between magnitudes was calculated for different optical wavebands which conveys the 'colour' of an object.

3. Mass of a cluster

i. Reject the outliers by plotting a histogram of radial velocities and selecting an appropriate range to consider. Let us assume that to be 4000-10,000 km/s. Create a subset of galaxies with radial velocity in this range and take the mean. This is the systemic velocity of the cluster ($\sim$ 6790 km/s[27]).

ii. The standard deviation of radial velocities in this range will be the velocity dispersion. (!$\sim$ 1067 km/s)

iii. The angular distances must be converted to radians by multiplying the values in arcseconds with $\pi/(60 \times 60 \times 180)$. The clustocentric distance in pc can then be obtained by

---

[27] *Your answers may vary depending upon the choice of velocity range considered. They are acceptable as long as they are close to the values stated here.*

multiplying the values in radians with the distance to the cluster (i.e. 10^8 pc for Coma). The radial distance, $r = \sqrt{(x^2 + y^2)}$. The typical distance of galaxies $!\sim 1.2$ Mpc.

iv. $M_{Coma} = 3.18 \times 10^{14} \ M_\odot$.

v. Total mass of cluster from M/L assumption
$!= 8.5 \times 10^7 \times 1000 = 8.5 \times 10^{10} \ M_\odot$. This is much lesser than the mass calculated using the viral theorem in iv., implying a large fraction of the cluster mass is dark matter.

4. Mass of a galaxy

i. $g - r = 0.54$ mag.

ii. $B - V = 0.75$ mag.

iii. $M/L_K = 0.63$.

iv. $K_s = 0.0827$ Jy $= 8.27 \times 10^{-28}$ W/m²/Hz.

v. Total flux, $F = 9.47 \times 10^{-13}$ W/m², and luminosity distance, $D = 15.6$ Mpc. Hence, total luminosity, $L = 7.2 \times 10^9 \ L_\odot$.

vi. Using the M/L ratio from iii., the stellar mass, $M = 4.5 \times 10^9 \ M_\odot$.

vii. The angular radius of the disk $!= 7.76 \times 10^{-4}$ radians. Hence, the disk radius is $!\sim 12$ kpc. Therefore, the dynamical mass, $M = 3.38 \times 10^{10} \ M_\odot$.

viii. NGC 4701 contains $!> 80 \%$ dark matter by mass. therefore it is a dark matter dominated galaxy.

AN INCOMPLETE LIST OF SELF STUDY TEXTBOOKS

- Extragalactic Astronomy and Cosmology An introduction *by* Peter Schneider

- Introductory Astronomy & Astrophysics, fourth edition *by* Stephen Gregory and Michael Zeilik

- Essential Astrophysics *by* Kenneth R. Lang

- Astronomy: A Self-Teaching Guide, eighth edition *by* Dinah L. Moché

- Introduction to Modern Astrophysics, second edition *by* Bradley W. Carroll and Dale A. Ostlie

- Introduction to stellar astrophysics (Volumes I, II & III) *by* Erica Bohm Vitense

- To measure the Sky: An introduction to Observational Astronomy *by* Frederick R. Chromey

SOME USEFUL CONSTANTS

- Speed of light in vacuum, $c = 2.998 \times 10^8 \; ms^{-1}$
- 1 parsec (pc) $\simeq 3.086 \times 10^{16} \; m$
- 1 astronomical unit (AU) $a_\oplus = 1.496 \times 10^{11} \; m$
- Solar Mass, $M_\odot = 1.989 \times 10^{30} \; kg$
- Solar Radius, $R_\odot = 6.955 \times 10^8 \; m$
- Solar Luminosity, $L_\odot = 3.826 \times 10^{26} \; W$
- Apparent angular diameter of Sun, $\theta_\odot = 30'$
- Earth's Mass, $M_\oplus = 5.972 \times 10^{24} \; kg$
- Earth's Radius, $R_\oplus = 6.371 \times 10^6 \; m$
- 1 tropical year $\simeq 365.242$ solar days

  $\simeq 3.156 \times 10^7 \; s$
- 1 radian $\simeq 206265''$

Dr. Smriti Mahajan

Email: mahajan.smriti@gmail.com

Cover: This stunning Hubble Space Telescope image of the Omega Nebula shows the glowing hydrogen gas and small amounts of other elements such as oxygen and sulfur. The nebula, also known as the Swan Nebula, is a birthplace of stars residing 5,500 light-years away in the constellation Sagittarius. The wavelike patterns of gas have been sculpted and illuminated by a torrent of ultraviolet radiation from the young massive stars, which lie outside the picture to the upper left. The ultraviolet radiation is carving and heating the surfaces of cold hydrogen gas clouds. In this image, the warmed surfaces glow orange and red, the green represents an even hotter gas that masks background structures. Various gases represented with colour are: sulfur in red, hydrogen in green, and oxygen in blue.

Image and description: NASA/Marshall Space Flight Center

www.ingramcontent.com/pod-product-compliance
Lightning Source LLC
LaVergne TN
LVHW061602070526
838199LV00077B/7142